BOOK WORMS

Our Holidays

Celebrate Passover

Amy Hayes

Cavendish Square
New York

Published in 2015 by Cavendish Square Publishing, LLC
243 5th Avenue, Suite 136, New York, NY 10016

Website: cavendishsq.com

This publication represents the opinions and views of the author based on his or her personal experience, knowledge, and research. The information in this book serves as a general guide only. The author and publisher have used their best efforts in preparing this book and disclaim liability rising directly or indirectly from the use and application of this book.

CPSIA Compliance Information: Batch #WW15CSQ

All websites were available and accurate when this book was sent to press.

Library of Congress Cataloging-in-Publication Data

Hayes, Amy.
Celebrate Passover / Amy Hayes.
pages cm. — (Our holidays)
Includes index.
ISBN 978-1-50260-239-8 (hardcover) ISBN 978-1-50260-244-2 (paperback) ISBN 978-1-50260-237-4 (ebook)
1. Passover—Juvenile literature. I. Title.

BM695.P3H3735 2015
296.4'37—dc23

2014032645

Senior Copy Editor: Wendy A. Reynolds
Art Director: Jeffrey Talbot
Designer: Joseph Macri
Senior Production Manager: Jennifer Ryder-Talbot
Production Editor: David McNamara
Photo Researcher: J8 Media

The photographs in this book are used by permission and through the courtesy of: Cover photo by stellalevi/E+/Getty Images; Jupiterimages/Photolibrary/Getty Images, 5; Clive Uptton/Private Collection/© Look and Learn/Bridgeman Images/Getty Images, 7; Westend61/Getty Images, 9; ©iStockphoto.com/JodiJacobson, 11; Oleg Belov/Shutterstock.com, 13; Ilan Shacham/Moment/Getty Images, 15; Photo Researchers/Getty Images, 17; Sean Justice/The Image Bank/Getty Images, 19; tata99may/iStock/Thinkstock, 21.

Printed in the United States of America

Contents

Tonight is the first night of Passover.

Passover is an important Jewish holiday.

4

Long ago, the Jewish people were **slaves**.

A man named Moses led the Jewish people to **freedom**.

During Passover, we celebrate our freedom.

Passover is celebrated every spring.

There are eight nights of Passover.

9

On the first night of Passover we have a big dinner.

It is called a **seder**.

HAGGADAH
for the
American
Family

ENGLISH SERVICE WITH DIRECTIONS

written by
MARTIN BERKOWITZ
Rabbi, Temple Adath Israel of the Main Line
Merion, Pennsylvania

11

We eat flat bread called **matzo**.

We eat egg and apples, too.

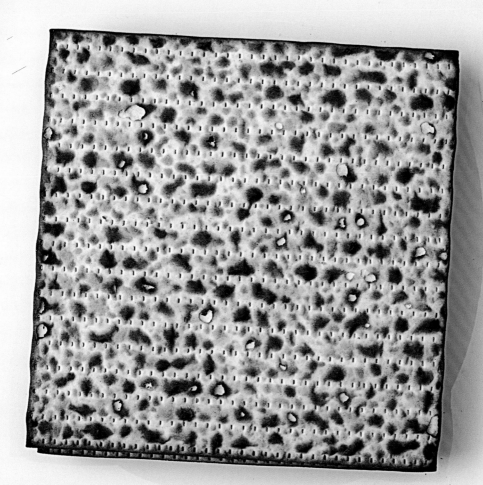

13

Each type of food has a special meaning.

We put the food on a special plate.

It helps us tell a story.

15

It is now time for the seder.

We read the story of Passover.

The story tells us about Moses.

17

After the story we have dinner.

The food is tasty.

19

Passover has started.

Happy Passover!

21

New Words

freedom (FREE-dom) Having rights and civil liberties.

matzo (MA-tzuh) A bread that does not rise that is eaten during Passover.

seder (SAY-der) A Jewish religious service and dinner held at the beginning of Passover.

slaves (SLAYVES) People who are owned by others and forced to work without pay.

Index

About the Author

Amy Hayes lives in the beautiful city of Buffalo. She celebrates Passover with her friend Sarah's family.

About

Bookworms help independent readers gain reading confidence through high-frequency words, simple sentences, and strong picture/text support. Each book explores a concept that helps children relate what they read to the world they live in.